THE BOOK OF SENSES

The Book of Senses

A CRYPTOLECTICON

Poems and other texts

Jeffrey Rocketmild Jefferson

ENCELADUS PRESS

First U.S. edition, 2023
Cover and text design by Patrick Barber
Set in Harriet Text and Neue Kabel

Enceladus Press
enceladuspressmail@gmail.com

ISBN 979-8-9880133-7-2

PREPARED FOR PUBLICATION BY IMPELLER PRESS
PRINTED AND DISTRIBUTED BY INGRAM PUBLISHING SERVICES

to Vicissitude and Egress

TABLE OF CONTENTS

The Light from World to World

13 Thanatations

CERAUNOMANCY

The Light from World to World

Now

these are the holy hours
I send you the emanations anew

in ignorance, grief & knowledge
I offer my prayer
a solemn solace

despite grueling eternities
offer thoughtful prayer within
a concentrated outward thought
to develop
powerful new realities

Epitaph

A slender, resplendent, cosmic Elf-Santa
in golden robes rides Haley's Comet
with his bag of gifts
among them
The Broken Circle of Absolutism
and other lessons
much too big for your tombstone

Bird's Eye

their celebration should not be modified
however, in my head, is macaw's blood
that drips symmetrically to the center

domino, maraschino
come to know
the meaning of the word
     flamingo

pensive in the router brow
in the dead cloud rain
deep in the flamingo brain
deeper than dream

feral donkeys digging
wells in the desert
where the night's lit up
by the phones of the dead

Temple Clock

with the clap of a tectonic eye
the temple clock
began again

drifting time-sapiens occlude the monument
though the point of occurrence
may never have existed

reverberate the spring, fall back
the clock has risen to the sun

I stand in my thunder-coated lightning eyes
as the shadow of my prayer crosses you in a song
inside the infinitely small distance
between now & forever

The Eye Socket God

searching for the entrance to night

I close my eyes and seek
I spread my sails & soar
out over the deep

shadows fall across the light that sheds them

the purple lion with a woman's face
jumps off the volcano into space
the trees I see the moon between

tuning up the rain for the spirits in the fog
they deepen as they rise, transit star crossed tracks
star trails lead off the Western hemisphere
descend into the Sea of Names

the riparian lion
appears in your nature
hypnotized by the strange effect
of water on light

you finally found your entrance to day
you finally found your entrance to night

you only find it once each time
inside, outside, its daytime inside tonight

doorsteps
doorsteps
doorsteps

rumble skull,
the distant sky's awake

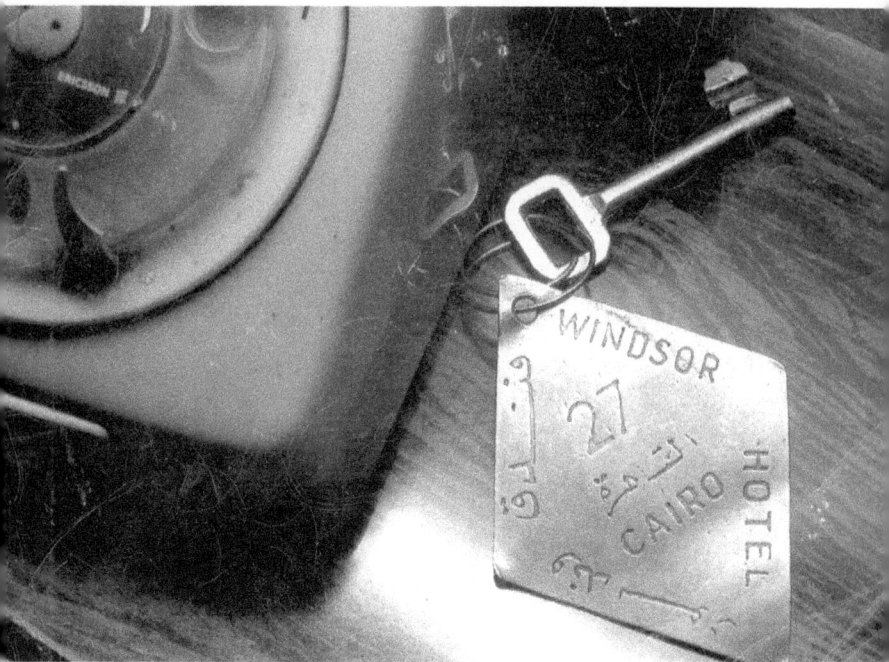

Zenith

the master STANDS
at the zenith of their power
casting shadows across
the ABYSS
I HEAR the music
and KNOW that it is REAL

Lock Unlock

lock, unlock
lock, unlock

LULU

Hieroglyphic Sleep-key Body Postures

the Floating Emperor

Mindbow

the Red Frame

the Boxwood Parson

Mind Pyramid

Moon

Dream Bleed

Locksmith

Clown

Shapes

Sky Graze

Eagle Egg

Cumulus

Soundwave

Arraignment

Blood System

Fog

Card Hand

Andromeda

Conclusion

Abatement

Rhema and Logos

Extinguish the flame, cast darkness upon the deep, for words are frail. Cannot the carpenter frame with more than nails?

there's always distant rumbles
in the corner of some sky
always dashing lights
in the corner of some eye

enclosed globe to transgress the threshold of eternal sky

elation beyond
elegance beyond
exultation beyond

there's a low bell ringing
deep down in the earth
traveling through your feet
up your spine
to the mind inside your head

elation beyond
 elegance beyond
     exultation beyond

The Sunglasses of Last Resort

burnt down boat for sale
like a bird with no wings
Bigfoots at the helm
of a narco-submarine

duende dancing on the rim of the well
conjuring bats flying to the sky from hell

piled under garbage with a bone-dry grin
nothing in the windshield but a Pious Jim
Babbling Brooke and sunburned forehead
Thirsty Baby Jonathan wants to go home

to the Life-or-Death Garden
of Geriatric Gethsemanes

Simpering Thomas made a portrayal of crime
his unspoken fear
that he would kill everyone
with a copy of his body
he's long gone

but that's the way I like 'em

clockfull of superfluous earths
extraneous cosmos
there's no such thing baby
as an unloaded gun
so don't meet the wrong stranger's eyes
might meet 'em again in the middle of the night

surprise is in the eye of the surpriser
it's the wet generation's cornbag Picasso
his face like a worn wooden mask
permanently foreign

Ouzo McCranius with his circuit bent clocks
Death's apprentice got Jesus' skull in her purse

staring into the sun 'til the endless message appears
it's time to feed the crocodiles
up on Parrot Hill

The Supplicant

walking in twilight's haunted beauty
bird calls shoot from the horizon
like comets across time

she confessed to me
her favorite unsolved murder:
"the Supplicant"

hiding out
in the woods and the sea

Coping Mechanism

paint the door beneath the shadow of the sky
the world we dream creeps through
and begins to be born

spirit money evaporates
eating aerosol cheese on zero street
at the service of humanity

the further we go the less we know
as we exceed the limits of the possible
what is possible is always in flux

the unsettling eye of reality collage
kaleidoscopic thoughts bleed
at the altar of sacrifice
for the sake of speed

images images images
we put ourselves for sale
upon the stumbling block

The Neon Address

cemetery mushroom
stone coyote
potent and perpendicular
I ate the duck brain
with my dress on backwards

make your blood stand still
walk on pins and needles

slow, slow, glissando
Gerber paste
across my sensitive bib

daytime girl
fingers one through five
beautiful equations and figures

now that's a good one good time Charlie
to be afraid of the number
666

that's a good one good time Charlie
to be afraid of
any number at all

out with it sick mama
blood blister explode
callous brain layer scar
ruby penetrate oxygen ground
diamond becomes coal
inverted stem
grow no more cold ablutions

ooo my baby what did you kill
this hog's gonna crack an egg in you

spy on the tablecloth while
the hose spool unwinds

clench your teeth let go and howl
sometimes a place just decides to go away

Surface

green conspicuous consumption
not just consumption

except they believe that all the plastic in the ocean
is the only thing actually protecting us all
from global climate cataclysm

dump it in faster!

we can just put a protective layer
of plastic debris over everything

preach the economic gospel
to a dead lake
in a burning forest

over do-si-do so
spin your partner 'round

extinction, like diamonds, forever
preach the petro-capital gospel
to the wet bulb dead in Portland

Nexus

I was pulled in by the Portal Power, and I observe the traveling souls gathered inside. They lay down for the pose & slay themselves upon the lens until the True God rips out the True Music their True Souls. They are wizards & time walkers and they jumped thru the jump gate into the late-night church of terminal alcoholics, where toads await & imbibe the transfiguring kiss. The Astrophysicist in his eyepatch, and the backwards key tickler, Donny the Immortal representing our Heroin/ Aids/ Racism/ themed professional sit-com sports team & here's my friend Intriguing Marcus. He screams "YOU'RE not FUCKing free. PANCHO VILLA was FUCKING FREE." And then when Kenny Cain gets off, he goes to pieces, he craves his mindless shame. Glory Gash in permanent distress delivers and amplifies sophisticated sarcasm with sadistic forgiveness. Yes, and the Corner Girls dangle their hooks. Like a sudden hologram on the barstool, with their penetrating looks. Later on, someone lets me take his picture while the skin falls from his distorted foot as the map of failure runs deep into the cracks in his fading skin, but the failure is not his, leaving me vibrating what he said about photographing the homeless as he hit that makeshift crack pipe and blew razor smoke across that bank window's vacant financial district glass.

Officer

& I told him as he cuffed me
I informed him

that I realized this was his way
of acting out a symbolization

an expression of his own bondage & impotence

that I saw him dominated
by something he feared
but could only partially perceive

forces that had possessed him
he was animated
like a tragic puppet
and I told him this
as he slammed me into the car

& I said
from the bottom of my heart
I feel for you man
I really do

& that I hoped he would someday find the strength
to recover from the hate
that made him so weak

Thank You for Your Co-operation

IN ASSOCIATION WITH THE STATE OF ALABAMA
TACO BELL, BEST BUY and WELLS FARGO

we proudly present:

THE ONLY GOOD SEX IS A DEAD SEX
and *THE PUBLIC IS EASIER THAN A DEAD HORSE*

(Because the weathervane never stopped spinning and the compass needle spirals holy terror as the final dispenser conjures terminal night horse blood crystal insertion)

Note: you will be fracked, you will be drilled, slaughtered, maimed and extracted like any other natural resource on slaughterhouse Earth.

Macroscope

O Human ordeal
no, I know no other way
bright lights go off in your mind
high beams

slicing sheets of time

Winter

Dim   cross

Death   frost

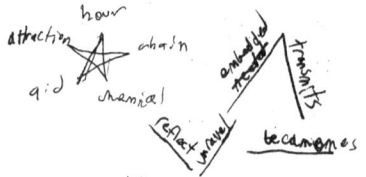

hour

attraction   chain

aid   chemical

ambushed/treated   transits

reflect/unravel

becomes

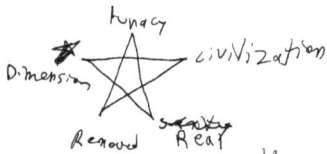

lunacy

Dimension   civilization

Renewal   Real

War

leader   sect

Amphetamines   fuel

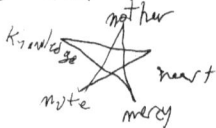

mother

Knowledge   heart

mute   mercy

Human

Path   weathered

Wood   nail

Penta-Star # Flesh

seal inverted corpse
nimbus blurts brother
corpse embodied inside
brother spurts concrete
inside flowing river
concrete spills mask
river enveloped mouth
mask knows iron
mouth disrupted seal
iron encases nimbus

Hour embedded aid

aid unravels chain

chain becomes attraction

attraction reflects chemical

chemical transmits hour

The Orb

relax
relax
relax, relax, relax

the Orb
is made of Silly Putty

Housing Wanted

Housing wanted pudding supper group home sex-dementia military fetish black hole. Bout ME: child spasm black magic knurled Hebrew gut sentence carving shithead. Please: near pharmacy and liquor store. cock-sucking bib splitters / bulb / splatterhorse. House rules no "costume jokes" / Mister Particulars. Food and animals. Plastic surgeons encouraged call now (777) gat-eway

Stampede

crazy horses stampede the horizon

scared of Nebuchadnezzar's
sapphire stare

Ad Nauseum

at the Cloven Horse Foreskin Removers Drive-thru
the paintings themselves were random
& The costumed wrestlers debate
where to smear the paste?

shooting the vials of Pope blood
at the Legion of Valor Museum
the speaker's ring finger ejects
a spasm of pink light

Numis Numatra creemus crouched
in Hogan's undercranny

the sculptress descends into the pit
spiral mimicry explodes
they are draped in wet sheets
of one-another's flesh

entertaining his castrated lust egg eyeballs
Mr. Faceville Genital Deathchord
the mimics spill themselves fanatically
all over her precision instruments

and the swarming mimics milk the mammalian truth
the absolver revolves the globular senility
they milk the mileage from the meat
& the mimicry compounds
even as the mimes mimic clowns
& she already shaved him and egged his mimic eyes
she clowned his clone & mimicked his mom
& his impotent lust egg eyes were scrambled
his political clown philosophy bled out limply

yes, the murder slime from the slime factory
which had filled his scrambled eyes
oozed from his wounded sacs of murder slime

regurgitating and re regurgitating
bubbling, grotesque, repeating
the thwack of the cleaver's redundance
with his dunce cap
involuntarily removed

GSTV

pulling up for a refill
at the gas station
pretty faces?

white faces
advertising
commercials for the next war
on the Gas Station TV
YOU know . . . GSTV!
"It's the nation's #1 'at the pump' station"

awesome stuff
fill me up with this
puff puff pass
love the commercials
advertising the next war

The Locksmith

In blazes of morning
the locksmith
files away the key
a six in the fifth chamber!

Satisfied with the numbers inside
the sequential chambers
of the lock

like a fine
surprising
poem

Discovery

I was 7 years old
the Christmas I found Santa
dead on the living room carpet

The toys were already lain out for me
my heart's desire
had been
a stuffed Batman

there was a note
on one of the stockings
what did it say?

They don't see.

but guess what?

I am a portal.

Into a cosmos
a universe beyond
even my own imaginings of myself

Ancient Flower

ancient flower
written in my flesh

I am the silence of Death
and a corpse that sings

Time is a Shadow Thrown

sit here
let time continue
do the work
and exist

Wound in my Soul

standing in the grocery store
staring at a wall of wine
all alone
my voice utters

"cadaver"

into the aisle
I laugh without control

at all of them
and no one

myself especially

Drop

egg in my wine
whole, submerged

really makes me think

it's no ice cube

The Sentient Letter

7 magicians of the wet chemical bless the lives of infinite sky
      (words in the truest octave)

written instrument conjures image to repair realities

execute alphabet research in the hour of right evidence
the intriguing sky reflection inside
the secret of the waiting Death Reptiles
in Earth & sky

Public putty spasm on 2 power spirals

ancient and sacred hand & egg alphabet
true body dissolve sponsored distortions

hieroglyphic bondage cartoon
DNA disguised in the changing dream
pulse the temperance code
recover toys left lost in the winds inside
Santa's black pyramid continuum
on the red horizon

7 works dried the wind 13
light into the house of creation

harvest, mirror, inflect, and amplify the cosmic word winds

The I among the ancient

Song for Mescalito (2003)

lay onto me the hammer of creation
mescalito's furious laughing face upon the clouds
　　circle circle of fury
　lay onto me your hands and your laugh lay onto me your hands
　　　and your laugh whirlpool of clouds

stirs my electric surge

continue your propulsions propulsions
your furious laughing face upon the clouds!

the breathing, breathing sky
raining sky, laughing sky
breathing raining sky, laughing crying sky
breathing sighing sky, laughing circle sky

wet dry wet dry so let the man thoughts pour forth
onto this device of man
what sense will it make to you?
let the man thoughts pour forth onto this man thing
let the light seep thru me

let it radiate laughing sky
look how his tendons do his bidding
thinking in the language of quick moving tendrils
care to see yourself age?
small sounds sound small sounds
changing sound changing sounds
small pools small pools
a force meant for man
a force meant for man
propulsions
propulsions of force
propulsions of force and explosions of forces

forces force propulsions
grace forces form graces
Fake forces form facades

but worse, worse, worse yet
alphabet which way the winds fly
but upon a page do lie
suggest a word?

forced against a wall of page with only words for weapons!
what force propel the words onto a space of page?

a man under a tree
a man under a tree with grass underneath

and beneath that hot earth
Earth breath slow birth

we all meet here?
we meet against the empty page?
what of your life will you scrawl
upon this immortal wall?

words
Thrown about by angry winds
danse macabre until the brittle skeletons blow away

like the words
splattered against the wall of brains

Mescalito you're a talented species upon this universe
a whirlpool vortex opens

Graven Image

graven image
graven, graven image

a cryptic edifice
bulbs, beacons
signs

we became the other's
Graven image

Well graven patterns have taken root, thought-space photon wireless liquid crystal brain trigger thought factory transmissions in the Untitled States. Feeding on media mirage, hallucinogenic hell nightmare of blaring schizophrenic mind cannibalism.

Those Who Have Come Across

A Cross, among the flashes of images in the Garden of Miscellany. A magnetic skeleton to proffer to you a human noise.

O Graven image

graven, graven image
a drop, a seed
a hand, a beam

The light emanating from a billion stars in the farthest reaches of inner space, a blind birth, a truly Original Face, in the eyes of the unshadowy sun, just before the Arc of Fear obliged us to the people, born in shadow, in reflection of the exploding star.

Graven Image!
graven, graven, image
but holy yet

The Light from World to World we shine it, both scathed and knurled. I trace the descending stairs into the rooms of the universe. We live in the trances, we live in the traces, in every thought, TRUTH, JUDGEMENT, SWORD.

To harvest the guilt and smash the word.
To smash the word is to smash the world.

To smash the graven seal. Earth as of this writing, being one of the more "diverse" worlds in this Cosmos, this "quadrant" certainly, according to certain outer intelligences. Somewhat out of hand they say, apparently, or so I heard

and what else might this image be?

Personal?
Historical?
Intuitive?
Logical?
Intentional?

A black ship on a black sea brings forth black cubes from the
dead country. The mind is a horse, ghost riders in the sky.

the Joker IS indeed wild
but holy yet

who can save the signal from the noise?
The source from the shadow?
Who can open the channel?
Who can open the lock?
Who can imagine how?

Possibly you
Possibly you

Use the magic Spells of the Alphabet, well graven and holy
yet, re-arrange them into infinity. The burnt offerings, the freeway
wind, and the damage.
the damage and
the graven image
The graven image & the superstition. Religion among those

with Business with religion.

carburetor, generator, solenoid

crop circle, orgone amulet,
pyramid, clockwork, piñon

The World
Temperance
The Star

circuit boards with spirit masks
space pictures, DNA
holy oils, reflectors, moss covered branches
dried reptiles, quartz crystal keys
burnt star anise

& the transparency of fire

Financial Eye

Impediment of the doom cycle, to crack open
the financial eye. Cycles expressed on black and raining
military fog figure, flesh usurper. Adam centers the
Tombstone in poison shadow to smash the extracted wheel.

potent SPINNING wheels of shadow
reveal vibrating mirage

The lights light the light of the living life, and the
undiscovered eye forms around the star. The active knowledge
seeps, bubbling Divine & screaming stone fully feels the awesome
scream of life.

white toads inside the child blathering evil.

O to the seed preceding the holy light so FREE!
Explosions of the sky bank, the bright united high abyss.

death surgeons supp the death wafers a trillion degrees
infinite of telescopic midnight

two more quotients for the toad

Full mind breathing cryptic mammalian plan for the
inner gift. Water witch, perceive noise chain dream of forgotten
immortal covered in holy truth present across the solistic
reverberations

body home and the CRYSTAL mind you tune

transmit the eternal nation's Laws

O realm, seed, zenith, lurching worse than DEATH
mouths the real ghost "was the room aware?"

To alter the Museum forever.

night air next

Transceiver

a ghostly message roiling in the drums
sleepwalking the barren fields
burning music to keep warm
on the human radio

Piano rains on the windshield
wet black street becomes a mirror
& the rainy wind blows
yes, the city is a funny place

bass below is throbbing hearts of throngs
human rights and wrongs
drums the brain-clock
the splashed glass refracts

passing neon cigar stores and moonlit bars
bus stop snare shot
city lights twinkle notes of piano rain

glass splashed by the dreams of the past
street mirror in rear view

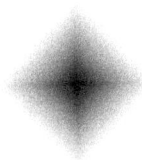

shows the city upside down
yes its a circus of death and laughs

trumpet is the wind in the mask of the revealer
Gabriel in drag
on the corner flying color striped flags
the tired and the true speak the unspeakable song
to which time belongs
so far out its in
so far in it begins
ringing the city air like a foggy gong

the note in the corner hangs a strange left
stranger in the jaywalk jags inside
the spectrum makes way
and buries the day
in clouds of piano rain refracting
moonlit vision
almost too miraculous to be played

as night was called day
the city night was eternal twilight
with telescopic music in all directions
as the street mirror moon soon sang
a new song on city blocks

over the hill the sun sometimes

rose and rang
the moon blooming
like a green light on mirrored streets
at night in the sonic sky
wet and black
sky star & brass
piano rain song splashed
among glass refractions

driving, but far away
sailing the boat that sails for years
fiddle blood ivory and bow
African trees, elephant tears
on the streets of San Francisco

temple bells
and the sacrificial skins of goats
vibrating spells
into the smoggy American air
full of piano ghosts

back East
in spiral staircase
face the haunted church
and the God-damned
burning cross

the singing blood
metal chimes of melted guns
melted souls and Detroit steel
rivers of hot metal blood and fire
grief and knowledge

shifting organ chords scintillate the foggy air
in tremolo temperatures cycling the hues of vision
black to blue
Squiggled lines out the horn
bend like flying snakes...

sticks snapping because the wind is pure spirit math
leaves follow math angles in the wind to the ground
while ambient air snakes take wing out the bell of the sax
and trace un-numbered grace like curves in all dimensions

Feathered serpents with eyes of burning emerald
spiral out of their horns tracing un-mappable paths
across the grid-world then into the dream

to the outside everything would seem plain enough
but interior is phantasmagorical fantasia
of arpeggiating crescendos and spirit vision
crashing waves of elation and bliss

the faces striate and become triangular

behind pink ferns the spirits blow life into the air

The bell speaks
what the reed reads
& the ear believes

Leprechauns jumping on the keys in fast forward
while Giants pound the bass drums in rewind
altering chords by inspection from another angle
Eagle eye fluorescing in the sonic wind
turning the holographic sound inside out
to search out Atlantis

I build the lost city in my skull
brick by brick in hyperspeed
propelled by manic pain and bliss
as eternity passes momentarily

Interlocking tessellations of tone code
instruct the sentient architecture
self-assembling indestructible temple
magnifying orders of intelligence beyond imagination

consonant harmonic scriptural elemental sound
in spontaneous crystallization
the lost city appears
levitating above the abyss

To sleep in the living river of sound
the river magnetized by dint of a magic spell
to dream far outside of words
to awake in pure enigmatic harmony
to dissolve in the fountain of peace
to die in the eternal giving of life
to continue the propulsive propulsions of music

transgressing concentric spheres of context
acoustic psycho-acoustic
mystic and beyond
sustained successions
of metamorphic energetic forms emerge
ancient forms yet individually unique

the music is psychic iron and steel
Tape hiss and bass plucks as distant piano creeps
wavering bass string with a consonant cymbal
piano tides arrive and consume the sphere
Slow floating brush on the spherical snare
bass laid back walking in the moonshade
piano chromatics adrift
faint as jasmine hinted breezes
from across the lake

body language sentence the cloud speaks

sky-strings dark behind the branches
vibrating moon mirage between
water waves reflected
on the face of the deep

bass of elegant spirit cursive in the longwave air
tumbling like smoke from the lips of Venus

vibes like ice across the top
two keys hovering in tight oscillation
while the band zigzags steadily advancing below
waves of knowledge emanating
trumpet soars like a cool blue seagull
with the perfect pace
the song is an ecosystem

the song will turn its gesture to reveal new facets
of similar awareness, proof of impossible shapes
jeweled thoughts, normally inaccessible
deepest inner realities made audible in the room

Pregnant with an Egg

Pregnant with an egg (through the naked door)
standing there in such a robe!
through the naked door and nowhere else.
in such a robe, pregnant with an egg

Someone who had never been anywhere before
not all or nothing
not all and some

maybe some and all
but not some nor none
but something begun
standing in the naked door
pregnant with an egg

take my buddy to Russia
take my friend to the end
pretend you don't begin
pretend you don't love us no more
cringe at the pretend Indian

get rugged on the rug and skin your knee
get bulbous with egg matter
get grand-feathered into the cuckoo
of the clock-faced hermeneuticals
get hella pregg with...

an egg

Naked Ape Before the 'Lectric Foam of Circuit Jaws

idiocy loves company even more so than misery
social acceptance through shared denial of reality
keep on refusing to understand
until you simply can't

binary syringe of lustful feral nurse
custodian of low urges

Human defrocked
disrobed of concern
barren of caring intent

harness their worse inclinations
inflame them, and profit

Funnel the resource onto the happy path, patiently let them
grieve their loss, exsanguinate, and extract.

Face

you may not know him by name
but you know him by face

well you may not know him by name
but you know him by face

face got 30 years
for hanging in the light like a broken crow
starved from surviving the night
he crumpled down in the grocery store

and the judge gave him 30 years

the song became the scam
God became the church
nonsense became the truth

and face got 30 years

Things We Saw

the Atchafalaya bayou
the Chesapeake Bay
the Mojave Desert
the Pentagon
The Lorraine

signs for "liquid country"
and Christ crouching in a cornfield
clutching a basketful of embryos

the Cosmic Ray Center of Utah
Window Rock
in the Hugeton moonlight

Lake Superior, Highway 61
the Gulf of Mexico, Route 66
the Bridge to Canada

a mafia bar on Staten Island
the Painted Desert, and
the Baltimore residence of John Waters

a mesa in silhouette
a dilapidated silver mine

the Smokies
the Appalachians
the Rockies
the Rockaways
the Great Salt Lake
& The Upper Peninsula

the continental divide & the Northern Lights
the Shenandoah & the abandoned Packard plant

the Bessie Smith Cultural center &
the Linda Hall Library of Science, Technology, and Engineering

the San Marcos the Guadalupe, the Blanco
the Trinity & the point at which the sleepless hallucinations
become problematic

the West Bottoms
and Virginia City's Bucket of Blood

the simplest thing can just expand without warning
like flying metal geese on a 50 ft eyeball
some corduroy road knock'em stiff and o be joyful
hundreds of original Ralph Steadman drawings on public display

in a public library

the City of New Orleans
the river of the world
West Oakland, Bakersfield
arctic vortex north of Kansas City
5 Mile Road, 20 Mule Team
Mercy Springs, nectarines
oranges pistachios almonds
the graveyards of Meteor City

Lost Hills
Bishop
Turtle Wash
Broom Wash
Searchlight
Crestview

Climax, Alabama
Murder Bay, D.C.
Two Egg, Florida
Slapout, Oklahoma
Correctionville, IA
Accident, Maryland
Corpse Pond, MI
or simply Weird Lake, Minnesota
Knobnoster, Missouri

Meat Camp, North Carolina
Zap, North Dakota
Experiment, Pennsylvania
Fingerville, South Carolina
Oral, South Dakota
Hogeye, Texas
Bumpass, Virginia
Camel Hump, Wyoming
Toad Suck, Arkansas

The Service

Churches replicate themselves with vulgarity down the hill. I know I must go through their bowels again. I enter, my mother bites onto my ass with vicious fangs like a wild baboon, and she won't let go. Inside, people are transported onto an irresistible conveyor belt of overpowering cultural programing, they conform to the manipulations out of psychological necessity, raw and powerful death metal bands entice dread-headed honkeys into Sunday school alcoves. I seek the basement beneath the basement, where a grey and reflective river winds between red rocks and steep cliffs.

I proclaim sovereignty with a voice from the wellspring, trance shattering action of significance, a symbol that ripples outward and across. I mentally flood the abyss, triggering oracular recall, a magic river with power deeper than our own. Scrying down to the symbols that breath into the vacuum mind, I see that the world is transformed.

Everything We've Shown the Mirrors

no horn
no horn
no wealth
no tastes
no self

love, acceptance
5 am, Los Angeles, another feeling
Oak and Madrone ash, scatter them

now you imagine it's time
to fix all these impacted hours, days
in the wee hours
when the night is old
your cold wrench is ready
the toolbox bleeds open
it's a hard confidence
you know what you know
when the solar door swings wide
it is the time out in the cold
you bury the silver hatchet

and open the wound

power is what is here now. Reconnect the relay, Roswell, diamond
eyes, there IS another way, as the chords sway.

no tiger

white is full.   bend.

Way Down in the Future with the Miracle of Death

so easy to smile and be beautiful when we're young
they don't see the old, hiding in the wings, ready to eat them
courseth the course, splatterhorse!

cut and return
make the flowers return
retrieve them from their starless sleep
shimmering in the deep from whence they bloom

The Etiquette of Insanity

the court & the etiquette of insanity

just another law-abiding murderer
just another law fulfilling law-abiding
law loving outlaw rebel murderer praise god
just another law-abiding murderer
cranking the gears
of the necro-political extraction machine

come with me lost into the doomsday clock
into a world of total illusion with
neither comedy nor redemption

got some questions?
you want to know what's real?
what happens when we die?
how should we live?
gold, crypto or dollar?
should our privates be concealed?

I think I'll just tie this flag so tight across my face that the blood is
cut off and I'm seeing nothing but stars, screaming blue life outlaw

freedom punching myself in the balls until they are so red, white, blue and swollen so huge, that they fall off, get elected governor, prove the existence of a white, Judeo-Christian jealous God once and for all and seed final knowledge of how HE wants society organized forever, and I'll give you a hint: it's machine guns

Come to Senses

broken mirror
the pieces don't fit
back together again

looking into the light of the bright sky
into future times
passing by I move like smoke
through the great preponderance
of memories and events

tributaries of blood carry thoughts
from room to room from limb to limb
into yet another of the body alphabet spells
life sentences drug beyond the pale
perhaps in the time of prophetic nightmares

oh! the tragedy of dream, burning absurd
in the starless deep
go ahead, tell it to me
and try to stand against the crushing weight of eternity

but I'll tell you one thing:

Lodgeman Transfigurehead
walks the floors
of the mystery courts tonight

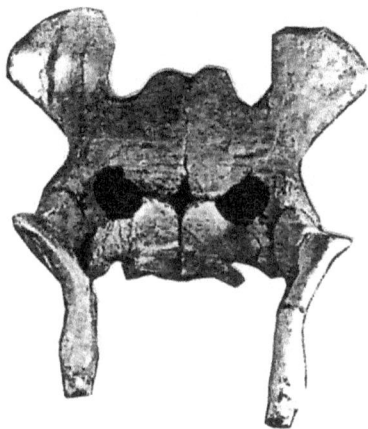

Somnambulist Crossword (Psychomagic Note)

an intimate enigma
a living being dances among the century's ruins
drenched in madness and light
fermented death perfumes
crack open the codes

broken open broken open
access access

broken characters in the comedy of existence?

now let us gaze into divinity

GAZE INTO DIVINITY
GAZE INTO DIVINITY
GAZE INTO DIVINITY

Somnambulist of the Singing Blood, black butterfly, amphibian egg absarakas in parallel fifths. Psycho-hypnopathic reptile brainstem, involuntary system registers objection, symptom erupts. Translated dream sentence, syntax obscured, prismatic harmonics. Gibbon ape fingers groping pleasure trigger attack, release, experimental animal consciousness, jungle consciousness, spontaneous symbolic action inferred. Airplane witnessed hovering midflight overhead, dead halt, 14 seconds frozen motionless.

Malignant things are caught in glimpses. Contract and disperse,
attack and release.

Events reviewed in reverse, newspaper mind, impossible posture. Recalled product serial number encryption date, time, location, working in the data mine. National Security Administration choked on its own ethical failure, non-distinct media demi-god myth rule illusion objective, Mexican soap opera TV aerosol botanica.

Hard bitten city music. Urban insect. Amphetamine veteran, crematorium, cemetery, death industry volunteer. Hospice counselor. Every night, re-write it, the naked sermon. Physical body chemical avenue of peering through life's limitations, obstacles pushing you to solutions previously unimaginable. Sudden oak death, aborted, truncated, abbreviated.

Somnambulist crossword. Necessary income. Chinese baby formula sales rep door to door axe grinder, Elthok, Algiz, Facebook, BBC, Al Jazeera, music figure, counterculture pornographer, flesh consumer, puff white buns are trash.

weird creature one of us

Biodiversity homogenization, homogenized diversity, DNA repository, ark of expired potentials.

Follow the Buffalo

.

Avant gauze weeping wound three-dimensional hieroglyphic blood coagulation pole dancing the imaginary Al-Qaeda Christmas party.

sarcophagus

.

The Kentucky Goat Man

it imitates the sound of wounded humans
but it cannot speak
a crying child, or a sobbing mother
this, it can do
at Pope Lick Creek
and it's decrepit bridge
their cry for help lures death
lightning struck the circus train
where Pope Lick empties into Floyd
a very narrow bridge
train track trestle screams
equine nose hypnosis
voice mimicry
circus freak
the re-incarnated farmer
who sacrificed the goats
makes praise to Death's accidents
thrill seekers, trains barrel down on them
face this monster under the bridge
the legend of the Pope Lick Monster
Satan made the farmer sacrifice the goats

then made him half goat as a joke

the pain is so contagious

they throw themselves off the bridges by the generation

the crying goat bleats like a dying child

the lightning strikes the circus train

the death toll rises

because the canyon cries

the farmer had to choose one goat

the Devil said

bear child with that one

lightning strikes the circus train

Fireskry

wild minds cry fire
cry sky
aye, the glassy ashes
kaleidoscopic shades
of abject black

Tempting Fate

NASA witches in ghost town graveyards
redact the mushroom cloud on mars
passersby go pale in the moonlight
Mr. Diego Time-lapse in the Diving Bell
found an end to put it all to
using psychologically refracted solar economics

ran psy-ops back in '67
a billion gallons of fear poured out of their clear minds

the sky is a time traveling camera that they live inside
disclosing actual photographs of the crucifixion
the people who turn the world upside down

space ache, buffalo gourd
the agony of space-time
await the aid
of the Universal Public Friend

Words like Blood Course Through the Universe

the blood of Christ is ALIVE
the blood of Christ is a program
Palestine, 1797
a flock of butterflies
the emotional feelings of the internet
the feelings of the ocean
inside a surfer in a video game,
the deity takes a job
the blood of Christ is hidden
the blood of Christ is spilled
the knife is a program
the blood of Christ matters
the blood of Christ shatters
deities these days become programs
the deity takes a job
same ancient energy
shifting in, shifting out
now a program, now a mass movement
the equations come to life
between believer and believed
science is a religion

religion is a business
and business is a science

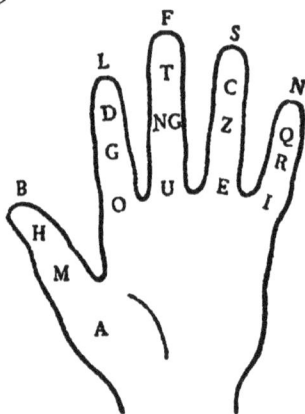

THE HAND OF 1,000 FACES

WRITES NOTHING
IN THE WILDERNESS OF MIRRORS

Lightning Love & Death

now the distant eyes of the foggy moon
weep lightning love
in the silent night

just as the word was abducted from your tongue
so too by the light of the moon
were struck the crashing chords of lightning love and death

dark days behind the mirror
buckling the horizon
with jattering chords of lightning love and death

the wounded healer becomes the mortician
and can cure the frown of the corpse
but lacks the ability to pass on her eyes

passing all potential emotions at once
upon the threshold of the two-way tomb
by the doors of the funeral parlor

inscribed with death's strange designs

the glimmering glass
reflects the blinding sun

the songs of the wildflowers
blinding in the afternoon eternity
roaring in escalating configurations of glory

with you in the indigo room
of the 7th lodge
we thrum the grand registers of the universe

13 Thanatations

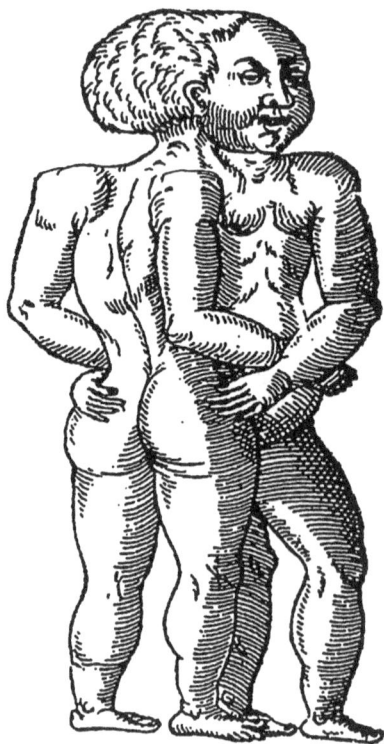

Children's Perversions / Reservoir of the Magician

Tessellation of Silver Hammers I jump within by night.

We offer this rebirth as a circulation to the faces of Truth.
They hand you slow illusion, transmutation, Disincarnate Ones

The children incubate a work
Sadism. Destruction. Divorce.
Wide psychotic grins.

hidden nerves and veins dancing into the Sun

The flow of psychotic forces. Paid mockery! The Business
Devil!

The Hungry Hoard of Soft Mammals touch my non-existant
song. Smash-phallus! Ruin! Catastrophe! The high heart of this
warm small mammal. Hot bloody ejaculation. Streak of skull
staring into the thought repeat.

Blood spattered tile gets redder with every strike
of initiating intellect and sexuality.

Awaken Descendent Nature's Habitual Amputation Ritual Eye

You will be in golden folds, aspiring to light inside a perfectly silent sea level.

what are the Power Angels at the Table of Death given?
Madness. Superstition. Eyeballs.
they exchange spoonfuls of weird religions
then replicate and divide

like Earth clouds viewed from space
they are dancing open the pillar of heads

Choose a symbol. Music. Perfume. Seven. The subconscious power soil.

Apes, falling along the banks, collaborating in the justice universal. They are adrift in waves of knowledge, grief, false prophets, fake priests, bridges toward their desires, harmony between judgments and inner fertility.

Do you know Confinement of the Emperor? Staring into the void as he begins to weep. Viewing the Inner Work. Obscure night facing the Beast of Cold helps the other to carry the weight of True Priesthood. Inspired spread of seed and coral symbols. The Presence. Can you hear the thoughts bleed? Light from heaven grips the domineering father. Images protrude from the Eye of the Ancients in the shaking basement far below paradise. Sacrifice to the Altar of the Wisdom Eye. New archetypes awakening, achieving unity. Four. His Diamond Eyes gaze boundary of body traced by cycle of mind controlling forces / fortune. Spiritual patterns are visible.

Ambient Snake Oil

I saw lightning thru the glasses of a schizophrenic clock salesman. On the sleeping pill, we are dancing in the slaughterhouse, the bath grotto, cathedral grove, organs of the state, at the train stop, mass murder on the courthouse lawn, the yard outside. The Liberty Dawn's Golden Lights of Morning Love, shining into the window striking golden trumpets slowly pouring blood from their bells, their harmonies are radiant hearts of golden sunshine reflected onto bloody brass. Grapes, Volcanoes, Pterodactyls, HA HA the drunken celestial beings are laughing!

I am Him Whose Name Was Writ in Water.

Embellish the Two Paths of Jail

I live in Colorado like I used to live in Texas. As a favor to Christ from Science. Death keeps his new poems unfettered by the trappings of Earth, in murder riddles grown during 1,000 year Halloween parade in mirrored transom. The future leaks from cracks in broken heads.

dead but not silent
veins explode behind sick eyes
doldrums stagnate souls

Behavior is a Neurotic Gestation

a beginning, those bells ring?
you desire infinite dimension

Sanity in the Womb of Night dances around the garden green.
Hearts through the Eye by the light of the recipient, in deep
intuition transmitting a work received through prayer.

(Green and black and yellow and white) Broken Scarecrow,
bathe them in characters of fire. Spirit motion of insect totem
cross. Messenger of fact astonishing in the Vast. I begin to extend
and see into a sleeping head like part of forces knives.

*My hair therapist pilgrimage alphabets float sacrifice to the altar
of wisdom eye*

Inhale blue fields above and below the Hexagon Pool.

The Hanged Advice

Light the Spirit of Successful Pyramids. Objects squawk and scream when their buttons press. For green glass makes algae grow. Do not mistake this to the world of perfection. Your face behaves like an Ape eating yellow shit. Try Stethoscope Five.

A Call from the Divine Deep

Spiritual folds in outer space continue flushing wisdom music into the ground. Irrigate the stream which continues through myself to the world. Gestation of the Given Virgin, Occult Church reflecting the green-blue concealment, bleeding out from the folds of outer space. Cross the failed, collapsed metropolises. There is a field of superior awareness just outside, giving off infinite back alleys of Lunachromistic harvest. Beware the call of the Police. Watch when they view cruelty more closely and look for radical secret blessings. Heartbeats under cycle, consecration, and eternal life.

Giant bees eat flowers and meat in homage to the Flourishing Upside-down Man. He exudes the characters of fire as Guardian Angel to the frigid man who is afraid.

Penetrate the blue-green fermentation, egocentric muse.

Astrological pattern on ground impedes progress.
Toast the end of an enlightenment.

progress move?

Carved by stream's evolution. NOMAD. ANARCHY. LIFE

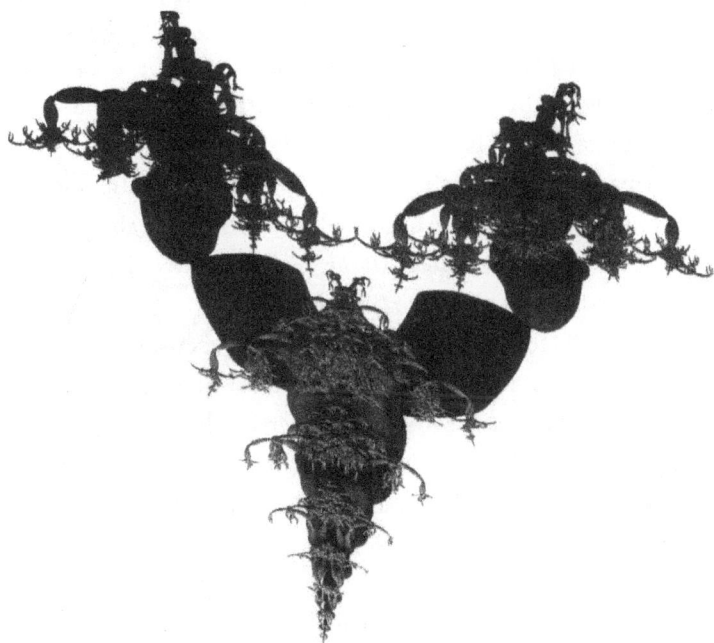

The Twisted Limbs of Providence

Prophets dress humankind in possibility. They eat multicolored inspecting lens to explore my intestine, reason, and my hat. Mind controlling forces fortune. Follow us throughout the swarming alphabets spurting urine on the screaming path. Perhaps you will find my spoon festooned with guts strewn about with song, but more to the square. The art under the skin. The face of one who fingers radiant frog legs.

Where shall I tongue the unbearable sawblade screamings? Consecration by pain. Rich blue fox feathers convulsing in a stream of semen. Electro-Receiver City descend to the songs bleeding out from her crack. A strict upbringing for all parents indeed. The She-Father. Daddy, grant me your book of drowning illusions, the essential of math and fortune?

"Pleasant piles of people law!" She shout bald.

Justice Lights the Trees on the Face of the One Who Can Decipher It

Revelations ground by the Universal Wheel of Immutable Laws. Interplanetary Music tearing open bodies to the Death Dance.

The brain floats in purification. Look into the Fifth Room! You can see into the sleeping head, fluent legs, desire to return into the eye. Absent of the tissue, the Three taking One's place.

Women on juices like alphabet soup influence the Aquarius Forehead.

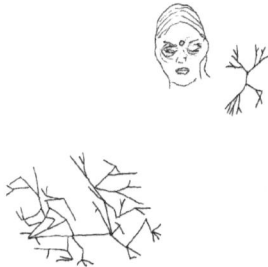

So You, Also, Total Darkness

"I was blind, bloody . . . it."
throughout the Aeon's Skull.

BRETHREN OF THE PULSATING BLOOD SKULL
gather 'round the candelabra, tambourine, and hissing cobra

SLAMMER!
(slammer of your future)
shake his hand and you will slowly die

Grind your bones and eat them
Boil your face off
In the holy water

Slammer . . . Slammer of your future . . .

Book of skulls
Rising from the water
3363.

Mission of Zotharis Carried by Their Left Hands

Dear streak of skull, born into this world

    in Jerusalem
    the poisoned prayers
    hang heavy in the electric air

    proof of productive wet flesh
    please expunge the liturgical dancebag

I dreamt of children throwing knives
riding their burning crosses on the Highway of Eyes
shining cleavers inscribe the insight deeper

they are the only clergy here

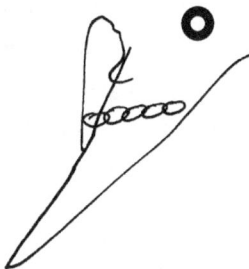

Face Behind the Waterfall Come Out You Have New Blood and a New Skin

I could not forget the electric delights of the God-reef as I grinned behind the wheel of my black inter-planetary ambulance. We're headed from Musar 5 to the keyboard planet. My limbs were heightened to receive the musical transmission. This planet is pock marked with station industries, it's just a stopover on the way to the fringe systems where we can find our Musars. The Musars of Musar 5. Magnetic Hearts wade through thought pools of facts, dreams and delusions looking for life inside the skulls and silent throats. We're catching some interference from the moon voice now, visions of the tides and sea vegetables in the back of my interplanetary ambulance. Mountains below us begin to dance as we receive strong musical transmissions from the Musars. All brain traffic melts away as the sounds sink in. Boundary moons, lunachromistic behavior, death dances. We are enclosed in a green courtyard as the dawn of love balances the violence eyes, life skulls begin to orbit our brains as the musical language penetrates deep in our psyches. Word angels are pouring insights over us anointing us with divine knowledge. We depart on a balloon trip thru the terrain of a bad dream which makes unidentifiable order in the head of twisted blossoms. Feeling extreme, looking naked, holy sisters gravitate towards magnetic rings deep in the comfortable power.

We meet in the Medicine Shell, fields of dead flesh in the distance. We must now cross the surreal exploding of beers. Projection babies are selling lust powder for fistfuls of payroll hours, and they won't back away until they are shown the screaming hammer of music. Summer's children are singing like phosphorescent birds in the garden of Eden, we are restful until the sky goes blind. Legions of brain worms are worshipping our sonic mind friends, the Musars of Musar 5. It's time to bring our bells and hammers to decipher the insect scrawl on the holy wall. A police spirit is flaming in the rain while the government drone twitches behind us. Massive rains in the senses knocked Marenko into hangover canyon back on earth and now the bosses alter stars in a church so the tide will claim the coastal trailer court. Dark instincts are sold by her smiles echoing thru the canyon dear Magnetic Heart. Sun walking river giants surround the river of guitars and one of them gave up a pass to the palace with some sort of musical vibration coming from the electric pool. Boundary colors are ringing out silently shattering perception and the vibrations are perceived not as sound but as vision, candles lighting of their own accord with intense polyrhythm. Beautiful holographic sapiens shouting "let the synesthesia begin". They are not Musars, but apparitions of the keepers of all special languages. The Intergalactic Treasure Revealers.

Have You Come for the Pictophilia Trigger?

Peeping Toms disrobe to urinate on a Branch Davidian's hair. The United States of male genitals with their deformed and monstrous attraction to bleeding wounds while the Middle East explodes in war masturbate to the patriotic cause. Beware Anti-Christ controller entity existence attractions to being eaten by Creature Voyeurism and making obscene telephone costumes under Food Somnophilia and sexual arousal from decapitated ghosts and aliens. Go do something Christ-like with your throat slashed.

crushed plastic in the eyes of sanity?

$\Psi_7(\mathbf{x})$ $\Psi_8(\mathbf{x})$ $\Psi_9(\mathbf{x})$ $\Psi_{10}(\mathbf{x})$ $\Psi_{11}(\mathbf{x})$ $\Psi_{12}(\mathbf{x})$

$\Psi_{102}(\mathbf{x})$ $\Psi_{250}(\mathbf{x})$ $\Psi_{500}(\mathbf{x})$ $\Psi_{1000}(\mathbf{x})$ $\Psi_{2000}(\mathbf{x})$ $\Psi_{3840}(\mathbf{x})$

$\Psi_7(\mathbf{x})$ $\Psi_8(\mathbf{x})$ $\Psi_9(\mathbf{x})$ $\Psi_{10}(\mathbf{x})$ $\Psi_{11}(\mathbf{x})$ $\Psi_{12}(\mathbf{x})$

$\Psi_7(\mathbf{x})$ $\Psi_8(\mathbf{x})$ $\Psi_9(\mathbf{x})$ $\Psi_{10}(\mathbf{x})$ $\Psi_{11}(\mathbf{x})$ $\Psi_{12}(\mathbf{x})$

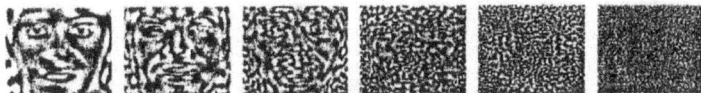

$\Psi_{102}(\mathbf{x})$ $\Psi_{250}(\mathbf{x})$ $\Psi_{500}(\mathbf{x})$ $\Psi_{1000}(\mathbf{x})$ $\Psi_{2000}(\mathbf{x})$ $\Psi_{3840}(\mathbf{x})$

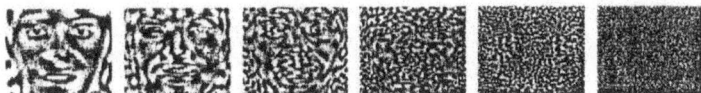

$\Psi_{102}(\mathbf{x})$ $\Psi_{250}(\mathbf{x})$ $\Psi_{500}(\mathbf{x})$ $\Psi_{1000}(\mathbf{x})$ $\Psi_{2000}(\mathbf{x})$ $\Psi_{3840}(\mathbf{x})$

CERAUNOMANCY

Aharen

its nighttime and the ocean glows
fluorescent electric blue
with blazing white foam
under the jet-black obsidian sky
horizon blind until the sky-wide lightning strikes

from Aharen to the Philippines
the lightning flashes on the coral reefs

a little seaside inn
the English name is 'Sea Friend'
the wind roars just like the sea

concrete stained with aging moss
bougainvillea archway
papaya and screw pine
stone stairs descend into the sea

telepathic sea turtles
flying in the ocean of night

between dilapidated shrines
where the ancient Pacific
coughs up the teeth
and salt-worn bones of deep marine dreams
beneath sites of war-time mass suicide
with chapel bells and lookout stations
above jungle tunnels
where moaning cats scatter
under bougainvillea archways
bridging moss-stained concrete forms
taiko pounding from the gym at the school

barren and heroic
as even here
they generate their crops of skeletons

gazing out the window where the taiko drums pound
with my whitefish and octopus blood

from Aharen to the Philippines
the sky is black, and the sea is blue

goodnight, good morning
goodbye forever
deep in the night of Japan comes the morning
it rains in every language, but the birds still soar

in the night comes the morning
and lightning flashes on the coral reefs
and the ocean rolls and the rain and lightning
come down on the life citadels of the telepathic sea turtles

it rains on Aharen and lightning shines
on the reefs of Tokashiki

at night
the Keramas silhouetted
by silent flashes

sky-wide lightning
from Aharen to the Philippines
on the black and rolling ocean

lightning illuminates the reefs of Tokashiki

I dive naked into the electric blue self-illuminated waters
under the gently raining black ocean sky
Kerama blue, deep in the marine lightning night

deep in the marine lightning night
at Aharen, Kerama blue
marine lightning night

Earth Fountain

from the seaside to the mountainside
the Beppu onsen boil
the folk magic bathhouses flourish
on the lattice of geothermal phenomena
as the steam rises from every crevice
like amorphous deities
casting spells on the town

Dimensional Almanac

I thrum the Grand Dimensional Almanac
to the page on which my own mind
dreams seven dreams at once

Monday, April 24, 2023, at the A-bomb dome in Hiroshima
browsing the Grand Register
of the Grand Dimensional Almanac
probing for access to pages on different layers

here is the guitar dripping with desert blood and sorrow
and another on which the goddess Strength
transmogrifies the face of the beast insanely

another dream in the City of Rivers where the sun falls
dreaming in multiple dimensions at once

my own infinite fractal chain of dimensional, exponential twins
dreaming together, living these stories at the same time
throughout the Grand Dimensional Almanac

I dreamed a thousand dreams at once

and in each dream
I dreamed a thousand dreams

all at once
in the City of Rivers
where the sun falls

Acrostic Chasm

O, I ambulate the cosmic street
across chiasmic chasms of the acrostic universe
deep in the human city

deep in the night of sanity
deep in the heart of the frigid alphabet
acrostic mind-glyph of interlocking cosms
across the universe insanely existing

awake, I ambulate across the chasms of acrostic chiasms
gestating cosmic soliloquy of acrostic lapse
fast passed the vast and lapsing cracks
into the cosm of the human universe

dropped in the laps of cross-legged
human skull caps, the universe gash
collapsed the lapsing void maps

castle of skull caps maps sanity skull sacks
across the lapsing universe

deep in the insane worship of skeleton generation
Anzosithross, my momentary dream name

and therefore, the gongs continue to sing
and the skull still shows in the larvae where they generate their
    skeletons

Hovel of Cosmic Scholars

the tongues are many
and the ideas flow from the mind of God
but the music is American

Bessie Smith in slow motion piano rain
the poster appears to depict some kind of Tiki Hitler

the wrinkled brow of man lusts after the boundary
the jungle and the cross you are nailed to with your brow

and when the music goes French that's when the lights go out
its tired and the blood is no longer symmetrical

the blood no longer drips in a symmetrical manner anymore
so shine the lamp down winding lamplit alleys of Kyoto
esoterica of the human stomach

they slay the sun, and they say the slang
they speak the token and the coin

they conform to the slot allotted

but the music will remain American
wherein the few scattered men
fill themselves with liquor and smoke
in order to contemplate the intervals

and unbelievably, the brush on the snare is the lead instrument
the Jimi Hendrix Zen kanji
the men mention Einstein
it lives in unfathomed dimensions

Herons

an island graveyard
rises from the rice-marsh

herons turn their heads
and nod

to spin the Japanese zodiac

A Foreign Sun Appears

tonight, a foreign sun appears
a guest sun
shows a new constellation of stars
in the galaxy of your brain
shows up at 2:30 am
bathes everything in an otherworldly light
othersunly new colors never seen before

in the nighttime turned day
a red lace opium flower umbrella
sprays its perfume
from a black and corrugated nozzle
hundreds of tiny spiral clouds
float before a brick garden wall

I form my mirrored knives
into a triangular window to the future

The Only Intelligent Weapon is Sleep

its nighttime in the sky
today, tonight
we chased the sun all the way here
and now it's nighttime in the sky

the circles we are in
from time to time
its nighttime in the sky tonight

written in water or carved in stone
all relationships can always change

the clouds are changing in the sky
mystery prevails

About the Author

JEFFREY ROCKETMILD JEFFERSON travels lands and realms creating and collaborating extensively in communities across the United States, writing and performing songs (The Lodestones, 3 Moons), theatrical plays (*Time to Not Emit, Kevin Pfibetto and the Great Pacific Garbage Patch Dinner Puzzler, Milking the Clouds, Last of the Line*), film, poetics, and sonic sailor's knots (Psyop Recordings). He also works as an audio engineer based in Northern California. This is his first book of poetry.